T0278435

EXPLORING **TORONTO**

KEN AND ETI GREENBERG

Exploring

TORONTO

A Guide to **28** *Unique* Public Spaces

Foreword by Amanda O'Rourke, 8 80 Cities

DUNDURN
PRESS

Copyright © Ken Greenberg and Eti Greenberg, 2023

All rights reserved. No part of this publication may be reproduced, stored in a retrieval system, or transmitted in any form or by any means, electronic, mechanical, photocopying, recording, or otherwise (except for brief passages for purpose of review) without the prior permission of Dundurn Press. Permission to photocopy should be requested from Access Copyright.

Publisher: Kwame Scott Fraser | Acquiring editor: Kathryn Lane | Editor: Dominic Farrell
Cover and interior designer: Laura Boyle
Cover image and all interior images: Ken Greenberg

Library and Archives Canada Cataloguing in Publication

Title: Exploring Toronto : a guide to 28 unique public spaces / Ken and Eti Greenberg.
Names: Greenberg, Ken, author. | Greenberg, Eti, author. | O'Rourke, Amanda, writer of foreword.
Description: Foreword by Amanda O'Rourke. | Includes index.
Identifiers: Canadiana (print) 20230227244 | Canadiana (ebook) 20230227252 | ISBN 9781459752559 (hardcover) |
  ISBN 9781459752566 (PDF) | ISBN 9781459752573 (EPUB)
Subjects: LCSH: Toronto (Ont.)—Guidebooks. | LCGFT: Guidebooks.
Classification: LCC FC3097.18 .G74 2023 | DDC 917.13/541045—dc23

We acknowledge the support of the Canada Council for the Arts and the Ontario Arts Council for our publishing program. We also acknowledge the financial support of the Government of Ontario, through the Ontario Book Publishing Tax Credit and Ontario Creates, and the Government of Canada.

Care has been taken to trace the ownership of copyright material used in this book. The author and the publisher welcome any information enabling them to rectify any references or credits in subsequent editions.

The publisher is not responsible for websites or their content unless they are owned by the publisher.

Printed and bound in Canada.

Dundurn Press | 1382 Queen Street East | Toronto, Ontario, Canada M4L 1C9 | dundurn.com, @dundurnpress 🐦 f ⊚

To Toronto, the city that welcomed us, with love.

CONTENTS

FOREWORD

WHEN I FIRST MET KEN AND ETI, TWO THINGS REALLY STOOD OUT for me: these two people clearly really loved each other, and these two people really loved Toronto.

These were my kind of people.

I met them in their apartment, a place with a stunning view of the city, filled with art and books on the walls. Eti, with a natural gift for storytelling and a kind of effervescent energy, told me about the long bike rides she and Ken liked to take on their tandem bicycle, exploring all sorts of places in the city together. Ken, listening intently, with an expression of endearment and amusement, peppered in interesting facts about the neighbourhoods they have visited, how they have changed, and how it all fits into the greater story of Toronto city building.

Since that first meeting, I've heard many more of these stories and witnessed this dynamic interplay between the two. Each of them brings a unique perspective, working in a kind of harmony and balance, not unlike how I picture them on their tandem bicycle. A picture of balance in motion.

These stories are always an iteration on the same theme: two people enjoying each other's company and the company of the city itself. The city is not merely the backdrop — it is an essential character in these little vignettes.

During the pandemic, I received emails from Ken and Eti. They were back on their bicycle and taking long walks, two of the few things you could do during the long periods of lockdown. They shared pictures and short pieces about the interesting public spaces they explored together. I felt like I was receiving postcards, except they were not tourists abroad, they were rediscovering their own city. Eti was often in the picture, standing statuesquely in the foreground. No close-ups, no cutesy selfies. The city is a character in this story, remember. Even though he was not in the photo, I could picture Ken behind the lens — his presence was there.

Later, when they told me they would take this collection of emails or "post-cards" and turn it into a book, I thought, That's a little love this city could use. Toronto, like many cities during the pandemic, was a ghostlike version of its former self, especially in those early days of lockdown. Later, we would see public life return in a new way as people explored their neighbourhoods anew, much like Ken and Eti did.

Toronto can be an imposing city, with its muscular buildings and traffic-filled streets. Our streets are still designed more for the movement of cars than they are for people. Being the biggest city in Canada and the financial heart of the country, the place where people from all over the world come to build a new life, it's a city that can draw you into a gruelling pace, where you can forget to pause and look around. However, Toronto, like many cities, truly reveals itself through its public spaces. And for all its faults, this city has some of the most interesting and diverse public spaces. It has beaches, ravines, parks, squares, markets, streets, rivers, trails, reclaimed highway spaces — it has it all.

I am a lover of cities. I'm endlessly fascinated by them. And to me, the way to really get to know a city lies in the little secret that Ken and Eti share in *Exploring Toronto*. To really get to know a place, you need to go beyond statistics or rankings. It's not about how many parks a city has, or how many kilometres of streets, or how many big companies. It's not even about who is the mayor or catchy tag lines. It's about how a place makes you feel. To really know how you feel, you've got to get out and walk around, and when you do, you experience it on a human scale. You smell the air, you feel the pavement under your feet, you touch the sand, you listen to the sounds of urban nature, car traffic, people on the street.

Exploring Toronto celebrates the power of public spaces, the places that connect us to where we live. These places shape our perceptions and experiences, influence our mental and physical states, generate spontaneous interactions, and spark new ideas, new relationships. This book inspires us to explore not only Toronto, but any city or town anew. It reminds us that we are not just passive bystanders, we are active co-creators of spaces — our mere presence in the space influences it. Our stories are intertwined with our city, each shaping our identities in exciting and delightfully unpredictable ways.

 AMANDA O'ROURKE
EXECUTIVE DIRECTOR OF 8 80 CITIES

TORONTO: WALKING THE CITY

SINCE THE PERIOD OF CONFINEMENT ESTABLISHED TO STOP THE spread of Covid, we have intensified our exploration of Toronto on foot and on our tandem bike. We would like to share some of our experiences and discoveries from those outings. The places profiled in this book are but a few of the many that make Toronto special for us. We are both immigrants to this city, but it is now the place where we have lived the longest and call home. One of the things we love about Toronto is its sense of immense unfinished possibility — rough at the edges, energetic, polyglot, and wildly heterogeneous, but also, at its best, welcoming, generous, and caring, trying to get better, and constantly attempting to expand its definition of belonging. It is not conventionally beautiful, but it has an abundance of riches: the lake, the rivers, the streets and parks, the ravines, but most of all its people.

We live in a city undergoing amazing change, and it has been endlessly fascinating to witness the changes in its physical form, take its pulse, and see the churn of new ideas as the city welcomes the world, becoming more and more diverse. There are great challenges and growth pains associated with that change, and we are involved in shaping it, trying to make it truly a city for all.

Exploring the city on foot or on bike offers a unique perspective and an opportunity to appreciate Toronto's detail and intimacy. This short book is our attempt to share some of the many places that have special meaning for us, things that are surprising but also familiar. Each of these is a memorable spot that has offered a moment, a view, or feeling and crystalizes things for us. Every one of us has our own version of this remarkable city we share. We hope you will enjoy this journey to ours.

ETI & KEN GREENBERG

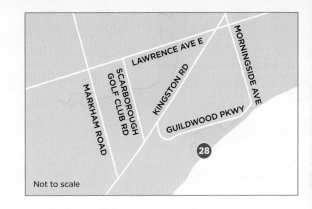

WOODBINE AVE

VICTORIA PARK AVE

KINGSTON RD

↑ GUILD OF ALL ARTS
(SEE INSET)

KE SHORE BLVD E

27

TOMMY
THOMPSON
PARK

26

LAWRENCE AVE E

MARKHAM ROAD

SCARBOROUGH
GOLF CLUB RD

KINGSTON RD

MORNINGSIDE AVE

GUILDWOOD PKWY

28

Not to scale

UNIQUE PUBLIC SPACES MAP LEGEND

1 Toronto Islands
2 Toronto Music Garden
3 Sugar Beach
4 Canada Malting Silos
5 Trillium Park
6 The Bentway
7 Canoe Landing at CityPlace
8 Puente de Luz
9 Victoria Memorial Square
10 Berczy Park

11 Regent Park
12 Rush Lane
13 Grange Park
14 Kensington Market
15 Front Yard Stories
(77 Yarmouth Road, 1016 Shaw
Street, 473 Clinton Street)
16 The Beltline
17 West Don Lands
18 Port Lands Bridges

19 The Don Valley
20 Trinity Bellwoods Park
21 Roncesvalles
22 High Park
23 Humber Bay Shores Park
24 Humber Bay Arch Bridge
25 Old Mill Bridge
26 Leslie Street Spit
27 The Beach
28 The Guild of All Arts

TORONTO ISLANDS

Another world
a short ferry
ride away

THE ISLAND IS ACTUALLY A CHAIN OF small islands that protect Toronto Harbour from the full force of waves from Lake Ontario. Originally a nine-kilometre-long sandspit created by sediment from the erosion of the Scarborough Bluffs, the peninsula's eastern connection to the mainland was severed in a violent storm in 1858.

The Toronto Islands are sacred land. For thousands of years before European colonization, the group of islands and sandbars was used for ceremonial gatherings and as a place of healing by the Mississaugas of the Credit First Nation and other First Nations. Eventually, the Islands became a summer resort community for Torontonians, with hotels, cottages, an amusement park, and the Toronto Maple Leafs baseball team's stadium, where Babe Ruth hit his first home run. An inner-city airport opened on the west end of the Islands in 1939. Many, including ourselves, look forward to the day when it may return to parkland.

The community on the Islands is the largest car-free urban community in North America. A long and complicated struggle over the homes on the Islands began in 1953 when the city decided that it wanted to remove the residents and replace their homes with public parkland. A Toronto Islands' Residents Association was formed to save the homes. In the end, 250 homes remained standing. It wasn't until 1993 when the Toronto Islands Residential Community Stewardship Act was approved by the legislature that the residents' future was secured. We are all the beneficiaries today.

The Islands are now an inhabited 330-hectare park with lots of room for picnicking, day camps, playgrounds, swimming, a nude beach, and, when conditions permit, even ice skating on the inland waterways that also allow boats to navigate the islands at other times of the year — a favourite pastime for kayakers.

The Islands are an essential place of escape for those seeking respite from intense city life. It is popular with people of all ages, serving as a welcoming place for Torontonians, especially newcomers to the city, and visitors alike. It also offers a vision of a different way of life as we try to reduce our dependence on the car. It offers a slower pace and a place of relaxation and closeness to nature just a short distance away from the busy city.

GETTING THERE

📍 Facing downtown Toronto across the harbour.

🛳 Ferries from the foot of Bay Street to Centre Island, Ward's Island, and Hanlan's Point; water taxis from a number of slips along the harbour; and, of course, canoes and kayaks.

🚲🚶 The Islands are ideal for cycling and walking. Bikes can be taken on the ferries. They are available for rental on Centre Island.

TORONTO MUSIC GARDEN

A grace note
on the harbour

FRONTING ON TORONTO'S INNER harbour promenade between Dan Leckie Way and Spadina Avenue, the Toronto Music Garden is one of the city's most beautiful and lovingly cared-for gardens and a treat for all the senses. The garden was designed by Julie Moir Messervy and opened in 1999 with the collaboration of internationally renowned cellist Yo-Yo Ma and the generous involvement of the local community. Its distinctive curvilinear forms drew inspiration from Bach's First Suite for Unaccompanied Cello, with different sections of the garden corresponding to each movement.

It was first conceived for Boston and when the project fell through there, Toronto embraced it. It is part of Harbourfront, which was created in 1972 with the purchase of former industrial lands by the federal government. The original development plans for the area were contested by the public for, among other things, not containing sufficient public space. The response was to move Queens Quay away from the water's edge, creating room for the Music Garden. If the Music Garden is the stage, the backdrop is a row of handsome mid-rise residential buildings designed by Arthur Erickson and KPMB Architects, with public uses on the ground floor, including a Music Garden Cafe.

We visit the Music Garden often as part of our almost daily walks to the water's edge. The highly diverse lush plantings make it a standout in all seasons, always appealing. The colours from the sky to the land and the trees dramatically frame the pathways with dappled light, beckoning us into the garden. The view of the CN Tower, a familiar landmark, grounds us. The monumental weeping willow tree is a favourite. Its achingly beautiful pistachio-green leaves provide a magnificent canopy — a treat for the eyes on this stretch of the harbour promenade and a backdrop for the stage hosting free, outstanding musical performances from around the world. We admire all the details, the special touches from the choice of the plants to the paving, the railings, the pavilion on the hilltop, and the maypole sculpture.

The promenade is a great place to take in the scene. Reminded of Otis Redding's "(Sittin' on) the Dock of the Bay," we enjoy watching the non-stop parade of all ages as we see how many others are doing the same thing. In the water and on the docks, the geese and ducks take in the sun, too.

GETTING THERE

📍 (479 Queens Quay West) Located on the waterfront south of Queens Quay between Spadina Avenue and Bathurst Street.

🚃 Queens Quay LRT coming from Spadina Station on subway Line 2 or Union Station on subway Line 1.

🚲🚶 Right on the waterfront promenade and on the edge of the Martin Goodman Trail.

SUGAR BEACH

A "beach" in a surprising place on the harbour

COMING AROUND THE CORNER ON the Martin Goodman Trail from the west, just beyond the massive Redpath Sugar Refinery, we unexpectedly discover Sugar Beach. One of the most interesting things about the city is its extreme contrasts, and this is a remarkable example. Always popular, this park, designed by landscape architect Claude Cormier, features a sandy beach, pink umbrellas, and rocky outcrops. Sitting on the Muskoka chairs that dot the beach, visitors can enjoy a great view of the harbour.

Claude describes his work as "serious fun." This sense of humour, seen in features like the umbrellas, adds a touch of magic. Putting your toes in the sand, sitting under an umbrella while watching massive ships unload sugar cane right in front of your eyes offers a unique sensation. It is really only half a "beach" — there is no swimming off the dock wall, but the location is very special because of the radical juxtaposition.

Sugar Beach opened to the public in 2010. It was developed by Waterfront Toronto, which was created in 2001 when the federal government, the province, and the City of Toronto came together to go after the 2008 Olympics. The Olympic bid was not successful, but the three-party organization was kept together to work on the revitalization of Toronto's lakefront, and it has been a going concern for over two decades. It has a strong track record of creating improvements to the city. Its strength lies in its commitment to "leading the area's public realm."

The triangular-shaped park extends right across Queens Quay to form a plaza in front of Daniels Waterfront — City of the Arts, which includes Daniels Artscape Launchpad, campuses of George Brown College and OCAD University, and a variety of other arts groups. A short walk up Jarvis Street and you are at the historic St. Lawrence Market. It sits on land made up of fill that was dumped there when the shoreline was expanded in the 1920s. Since then, change has been a constant. The harbour was used for industrial purposes for most of the twentieth century — the sugar refinery is a remnant of the kind of operations found there.

Only recently has the waterfront found a new life. It is opening up with new residential and mixed-use neighbourhoods and parks. Public access to the waterfront is now being developed. Sugar Beach, previously a parking lot, is a key piece of this transformation. It is a gateway to the water's edge promenade, which will eventually wrap the entire harbour and the new Queens Quay with its generous pedestrian and cyclist "greenway."

GETTING THERE

📍 Located on the south side of Queens Quay on the east side of the Jarvis Street Slip.

🚊 Queens Quay LRT (currently only to the foot of Bay Street), Number 75 Sherbourne Street bus.

🚲🚶 Right on the Martin Goodman Trail.

CANADA MALTING SILOS

New life for a historic landmark on Toronto Harbour

TWO MONUMENTAL SILOS BOOKEND Toronto Harbour: the Canada Malting silos at the foot of Bathurst Street and the Victory Soya Mills silos at the foot of Parliament Street. Given their scale and prominence, this pair have vital new roles to play in a revitalized waterfront. Every time we walk along the water by the Music Garden, we try to imagine what the future use of the Canada Malting silos might be.

The Canada Malting silos, built in 1928 at the height of Toronto's early twentieth-century industrial expansion, were abandoned in the 1980s. They have somehow survived, legacies of a past of which few other traces remain. Over the years, there have been numerous plans for their adaptive reuse, but there were difficulties: deterioration of the structures, finding the right combination of uses, and arranging financing. The timing for repurposing them may now be right.

Their heritage status has been acknowledged, and a program of rehabilitation began in late spring 2021. There is enormous potential for public use.

There are two distinct parts to the Canada Malting silos. The central opening between them is being opened up as a gateway to the water's edge. The night lighting of the silos will give Toronto a gleaming, glowing western bookend for the harbour. When the structural rehab on the silos is finished, the fences will come down and a great new park will be created around the base. This is part of the larger Bathurst

Quay Neighbourhood Plan, approved in 2017, which aims to improve the surrounding unused city-owned property with new public spaces, including a promenade connection to Ireland Park. There is a plan to eventually turn the silos into a cultural and community services hub and destination on the harbour. OCAD University has already been engaged with plans to use the silos to facilitate critical dialogues on climate resilience through the lens of art and design and will include activities such as public arts programming, exhibitions, installations, and symposiums, done in collaboration with Indigenous, local, national, and international partners.

The start of refurbishment of these long-neglected structures is a hopeful sign of renewal connecting past, present, and future. It is encouraging to see that similar plans are being developed for the Victory Soya Mills silos at the other end of the harbour. The pieces are falling into place to reconnect the waterfront from the central harbour to Port Lands and the new mouth of the Don River.

GETTING THERE

9 Eireann Quay.

The silos are a short walk from the stop on the Queens Quay LRT lines from Union Station on subway Line 2, the Exhibition, and at the foot of Bathurst Street.

The Martin Goodman Trail on the waterfront passes right by.

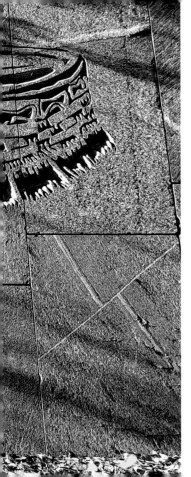

TRILLIUM PARK

A renewed vision
for Ontario Place

ONTARIO PLACE WAS CREATED AS A bold new form of waterfront public park to showcase Ontario, just as the islands built for Expo 67 in Montreal had done for Canada. Now that vision has been challenged, and there is an ongoing argument about its future. A proposal has been put forward to transform Ontario Place into a kind of theme park dominated by private sector attractions. We are members of Ontario Place for All, an advocacy group that has joined forces with other organizations working to ensure the preservation of the legacy created by architect Eberhard Zeidler and landscape architect Michael Hough, but most importantly to show how this legacy can be incorporated in a future that responds to the

tremendous need for public space in our growing city and becomes a vital link in the plans for the larger waterfront.

Trillium Park opened in 2017 and is a demonstration of what is possible. Designed by landscape architect Walter Kehm of LANDinc in collaboration with West 8 from Rotterdam, it wraps the eastern edge of Ontario Place. The William G. Davis Trail (named for the former premier who opened Ontario Place in 1971) weaves through its three hectares of naturalized landscape. The park consists of trails, rolling landforms, rock outcrops, firepits, and pebble beaches, and offers spectacular views of the city and the open lake. Because of its topography, the park feels much bigger than it is. From the grassy slopes and the trail, you see planes, boats, joggers, walkers, cyclists, and in-line skaters all enjoying the big sky and the open horizon.

There is a rich mix of vegetation: Ontario trees including red oak, red pine, and sugar maple "marker trees" can be found, along with shrubs and perennials, including highbush cranberry, wild ginger, and St. John's wort. The marker trees are a traditional First Nations' way of navigation, created by forcing the young trees to grow with two ninety-degree bends in the trunk.

We especially love the Moccasin Identifiers, designed with the Mississaugas of the Credit, etched in the stone walls of the "ravine" passing under a pedestrian/ cycle bridge at the threshold to the park. Another of the really special features is the re-creation of a rock bluff that uses granite slabs from northern Ontario, which creates a great climbing wall for adventurous kids.

GETTING THERE

♥ (955 Lake Shore Boulevard West) Hugging the eastern edge of Ontario Place south of Lake Shore Boulevard.

🚇 A short walk south from the Queens Quay LRT stop at the Princes' Gates entrance to Exhibition Place.

🚲🚶 Easy access from the Martin Goodman Trail.

THE
BENTWAY

A treasure hiding
in plain sight

IN APRIL OF 2015, WE WENT FOR A walk under the Gardiner Expressway west of Bathurst Street with our friends Judy and Wil Matthews to discuss the idea of transforming the abandoned no man's land under the elevated highway. Watching the neighbourhood evolve, Ken had written a piece for the Friends of Fort York's journal four years earlier suggesting that the space under the highway, and the roughly sixteen hectares of Fort York beside it, could become a kind of central park for all the new development occurring in this former industrial area. Judy and Wil loved the idea, and, in an extraordinary act of civic generosity, they partnered with the City of Toronto to make the idea a reality.

Designed by the very talented landscape architecture firm Public Work working with Ken, the first phase occupies more than four hectares stretching 610 metres from just west of Strachan Avenue to Fort York Boulevard. The space, defined by the monumental concrete "bents" (the combined columns and beams holding up the highway), has a grand and noble quality and possesses a kind of strange beauty, contrasting with the green slope of the historic fort on its edge. Despite its location, it feels surprisingly safe and comfortable.

It is a place for all seasons and all ages, with a 220-metre, figure-eight skating trail in winter and all manner of programming throughout the year forming a great civic living room for the over 125,000 residents nearby to the visitors who use the many amenities and attend one-of-a-kind performances and art installations. There is always something new to discover.

The Bentway is a vital city connector, tying together Fort York and its visitor centre, all the surrounding new neighbourhoods, and the waterfront a short distance away. From the new Garrison Crossing bridges that connect the Bentway to Stanley Park across the rail corridor a panoramic view of the city is revealed. This is just the beginning, and we continue to anticipate each next move as the "Bentway Corridor" stretches out from Exhibition Place to the Don River, converting more "found spaces" into vibrant community places, and plays host to a range of new cultural programming. The Bentway has pioneered a conservancy model for Toronto that is being replicated in other places.

GETTING THERE

◉ Adjacent to Fort York, it stretches from Strachan Avenue to Fort York Boulevard under the Gardiner Expressway.

🚊 The Bathurst streetcars and the Queens Quay 509 LRT are all close by.

🚲🚶 Not far from the Martin Goodman Trail to the south; can be accessed from the Garrison Crossing bridge pedestrian cycle route from Stanley Park to the north.

CANOE LANDING AT CITYPLACE

A red canoe anchors
a new high-rise
neighbourhood

RARELY DOES A WORK OF PUBLIC ART define a whole neighbourhood. The *Red Canoe* by Douglas Coupland, situated on an elevated bluff in its namesake park, with a panoramic view of the city, does just that. Designed by landscape architects PFS Studio of Vancouver in collaboration with the Planning Partnership of Toronto, Canoe Landing Park serves as the heart of CityPlace and is one of the most used parks in the city. This new neighbourhood, within walking distance of the downtown core, occupies land that once housed marshalling yards and roundhouses for the Canadian National and Canadian Pacific Railways.

When Ken worked for the city in the 1980s, he contributed to a master plan to redevelop this large site with the aim of filling in a gap between the historic city north of Front Street and the harbour with a mixed-use, mixed-income community. We were originally skeptical as we watched this dense high-rise neighbourhood with 7,500 residential units eventually housing eighteen thousand people take shape, but as we began to walk it and know it, as we saw it become a real neighbourhood, we changed our minds.

The gap has now been filled in, and the neighbourhood is well connected on all sides to its neighbours. The three-and-a-quarter-hectare park serves as a real heart for the neighbourhood, offering a place of recreation for residents and attracting visitors, too. We often make a point to walk through it on our way to the lakefront.

There is something for everyone. The artificial turf pitch is always full of life, hosting activities of all kinds from pickup soccer games to groups exercising or doing martial arts. Lots of kids learn to ride their bikes and scooters in the park's safe area with no cars. Another Douglas Coupland art piece, enormous colourful fishing "bobbers," creates a space for water play next to a playground with convenient seating for parents and grandparents.

Across Fort York Boulevard there are pubs and outdoor cafés; a supermarket; the Fort York Library, which is our local branch; and an eclectic row of live-work units for small independent businesses. There is a mix of social housing and market-priced housing. The Bentway's offices are in the community centre overlooking the park and a trail connecting to the Bentway extends along its southern edge.

GETTING THERE

📍 Between Fort York Boulevard and Lake Shore Boulevard east of Dan Leckie Way.

🚋 The Bathurst streetcar and the Spadina LRT are close by.

🚲🚶 The park can be accessed via all the surrounding streets, including Fort York Boulevard, the Bathurst Street bridge from the north, the Puente de Luz bridge from Portland Street, and the Spadina Avenue bridge over the rail corridor.

PUENTE DE LUZ (THE "YELLOW BRIDGE")

A vital link overcoming a divide

THIS BRIDGE IS ONE OF OUR FAVOUR-
ite places. We can see it from our home,
and we walk and bike it often. It connects
us to our neighbours in CityPlace and to
the waterfront. It is magnificent when lit
up at night with the backdrop of city lights
and the CN Tower.

Before this bridge was in place, the
CityPlace community to the south of the
rail corridor was very poorly connected to
the growing neighbourhood of Wellington
Place to the north. The two sides are separ-
ated by one of the largest and most active
rail corridors in Canada. What a difference this bridge has made in overcoming
the solitudes and divisions, redrawing the
city map. The pedestrian and cycle flow
back and forth over the rail corridor is now
almost constant as the city grows denser on
both sides. The frequency of bridge crossings — the Spadina bridge, the Puente de
Luz, and the historic Bathurst Street truss
bridge — show how increasingly important these have become in stitching the city
together.

To further reduce the barrier created by
the rail corridor, the city put forward an
ambitious proposal for a "rail deck park" to
cover the corridor from Bathurst Street to
east of Spadina Avenue, but developers won
the right to build on part of the corridor.
We are still hoping for a partial "rail deck,"
with green space over the tracks, which is
essential to serve the growing population.

Five metres wide and 125 metres
long, the bridge was designed by Chilean

sculptor Francisco Gazitua in collaboration with engineers Peter Sheffield and the MMM Group. It opened in 2011. The name, *Puente de Luz* (Bridge of Light), was chosen by the sculptor to signify the link between the north and south, the two countries that collaborated to build it — Canada and Chile. It is sculptural, with a playful dragon motif suggesting a tail and head. Some have described it as "the largest public art installation in Canada." It is yellow, hence our nickname, and we love the bright colour against a backdrop of otherwise greyish condo towers.

Whenever we cross the bridge, we enjoy watching the trains passing below and we are not the only ones. We notice many parents who take their kids onto the bridge for train watching. Also, many photographers use it as vantage point to show how the city is dramatically changing all around.

GETTING THERE

📍 Located over the rail corridor on the axis of Portland Street to the north and Dan Leckie Way to the south between Bathurst Street and Spadina Avenue.

🚆 Not far from stops on the Spadina LRT, the Bathurst streetcar, and the King streetcar.

🚲🚶 Access from local streets on both sides of the corridor.

VICTORIA MEMORIAL SQUARE

A multi-layered oasis in
the heart of the city

WE MOVED INTO AN APARTMENT ON the edge of Victoria Memorial Square in 1998. At the time, the square was virtually abandoned, but as we soon discovered, it had fascinating stories to tell.

The square was originally the burial ground for Fort York, and it still had five hundred unmarked graves. Eventually, a new vision for the space emerged. In 1837 a plan for the westward expansion of the growing young city using the "military reserve" was developed. This new area, Wellington Place, was to incorporate three squares — Victoria and Clarence connected by a grand Wellington Street boulevard, and St. Andrews — modelled on the west end of London.

This 185-year-old plan has seen many changes, including the arrival in the mid-nineteenth century of the railways, which brought a wave of handsome factories and warehouses, including the garment industry. These industries departed in the mid-twentieth century, moved out by globalization. Zoned for industrial use, no residences were allowed there. Instead, parking lots proliferated.

In the 1990s, an effort that Ken participated in with Jane Jacobs and newly elected mayor Barbara Hall opened the door to mixed-use zoning. Victoria Memorial Square is today a national historic site linked to Fort York. There is a memorial to the War of 1812 by celebrated Canadian sculptor Walter Seymour Allward, and through an initiative of the newly formed Wellington Place Neighbourhood

Association, the burial ground has been delineated with granite pavers.

The square is now the focus of a remarkable renaissance, as downtown has repopulated and all its edges have been reclaimed with new mixed-use buildings, including ours. The neighbourhood is becoming livelier, and all daily needs can now be met within easy walking distance. The square itself has become a busy pedestrian crossroads, linked to the waterfront, and a popular destination for residents and visitors. This was extremely evident during Covid, when it served as an outdoor living room. Its use made it clear that we need more public space to serve the growing population.

We are involved in the improvement plans underway to relieve the pressures and provide a close-by area for dogs and an enlarged playground for mixed ages. We have a front-row seat from our balcony that allows us to observe all these changes and we are continually working with our neighbours to shape what comes next.

GETTING THERE

📍 (10 Niagara Street) Located in a square formed by Wellington Street West, and Portland and Niagara Streets.

🚋 King streetcar (Portland and Bathurst Streets stops), Bathurst streetcar (Niagara Street stop), and Spadina LRT (King Street West and Front Street West stops).

🚲🚶 Local streets

BERCZY PARK

The "dog fountain" in the middle adds a touch of "serious fun"

THIS DELIGHTFUL LITTLE PARK IS LO-cated in the triangle formed where Front Street, which follows the shoreline, meets Wellington Street, one of the streets laid out in the grid pattern that is typical of much of the old city. The east end of the park is framed by a well-loved mural by the artist Derek Michael Besant paint-ed on the rear facade of the city's icon-ic Gooderham Building or, as it is more generally known, the Flatiron Building. The park is named after William Berczy, a multi-talented entrepreneur, architect, and surveyor who collaborated in the 1790s with John Graves Simcoe, first lieutenant governor of Upper Canada and founder of its capital, York, the town that grew to become Toronto.

Berczy Park was a parking lot when Ken founded the city's first Urban Design Group in the late 1970s. One of the group's first assignments was to transform the St. Lawrence area into a mixed-use lived-in neighbourhood by adding new public spaces and removing traffic lanes to widen sidewalks. Apart from a few notable histor-ic structures, such as the heritage cast-iron facade buildings that had survived across from the park on Front Street, the area was barren, a desert of parking lots serving the office concentration in the financial district at King and Bay Streets. Among the Urban Design Group's first projects was the cre-ation of Berczy Park, which opened in 1980.

As the neighbourhood became more densely populated, the park was heavily used and needed a facelift. It was redesigned by landscape architect Claude Cormier of Montreal. His welcoming design includes as its centrepiece the "dog fountain" — another touch of "serious fun" and whimsy — in the middle of a generous crossroads plaza. Its two-tier fountain has cast-iron statues of twenty-seven dogs and one cat. The dogs, spouting jets of water from their mouths, are all looking up toward a large bone perched on the fountain's peak. It is a magnet for kids.

With its long comfortable benches and loose tables and chairs, the park is an oasis, a perfect place for all ages to enjoy each other's company and watch the parade of life. Its trees provide dappled shade. Musicians are invited to set up and entertain. It is a perfect setting for performers like the Dauntless City Theatre company, which presented Shakespeare's *All's Well That Ends Well* in the park, inviting the audience to follow the actors in an outdoor, ambulatory production.

GETTING THERE

35 Wellington Street East.

A short walk east of King or Union subway stations and south of the King streetcar.

The adjacent roads are often choked with traffic, but the park can be accessed from Wellington, Front, Church, and Scott Streets.

REGENT PARK

From isolation
to integration

WHEN STANDING IN THE MIDDLE OF Regent Park with its new two-and-a-half-hectare central park and new shops and community amenities on Dundas Street, you feel like you're in just another typical city neighbourhood. It wasn't always the case.

Regent Park was created after the Second World War when an older working-class neighbourhood, seen as a "slum," was demolished to make way for a new self-contained public housing project. The plan did away with city streets, creating in their place two large internalized "super-blocks" with a mix of three-storey walk-up brick buildings, two-storey townhouses, and five high-rise towers. The buildings were lean and mean, "spartan," and, despite its grand name, there was not really a park in Regent Park. However, despite the poor physical environment, the neighbourhood, which was a major point of arrival for new immigrant communities, was culturally rich.

Thanks to a massive effort, Regent Park has been reconnected to its neighbours, and it is now arguably one of the best-equipped neighbourhoods in the city for kids. With residents coming from every corner of the globe, it is an appealing model of what a neighbourhood in our remarkably diverse and heterogeneous Toronto can look and feel like. It also represents an important evolution in Toronto's approach to low-income housing.

By 2002, after a number of failed attempts, Toronto Community Housing and the city embarked on an ambitious revitalization plan to transform Regent Park from an isolated public housing project to an integrated mixed-income neighbourhood. Ken began work on the revitalization plan for Toronto Community Housing with an extensive community engagement process. The plan took many cues from the St. Lawrence neighbourhood, a successful example of mixed-use and mixed-income housing. It combines high-rise, mid-rise, and townhouses, with different architects for each building. Market-rate and subsidized housing are checkered throughout, and it is impossible to tell the difference — no stigmatizing.

Dundas and Parliament Streets are now lined with shops and draw people from around the city. The plan is being implemented in phases. The constant key to success has been the parallel social development program that has produced such things as the Daniels Spectrum, an arts complex, the Pam McConnell Aquatic Centre, a new community centre, and the refurbished Nelson Mandela Park Public School.

GETTING THERE

Located between River Street, Parliament Street, Gerrard Street, and Shuter Street.

Dundas streetcar, Parliament bus, and College streetcar lines.

Bike lanes on Dundas Street, River Street, Shuter Street, and neighbourhood streets.

RUSH LANE (A.K.A. "GRAFFITI ALLEY")

An open-air gallery for remarkable street art

RUSH LANE, ALSO KNOWN AS Graffiti Alley, is famous, having served as the locale for Rick Mercer's walking rants in his TV show *The Mercer Report*. With its many murals, some of which cover the walls of entire buildings, the alley is a captivating outdoor gallery of great street art, drawing visitors from all around the world.

In the alley's early days, painting on the walls was illegal, so graffiti artists would usually create their works in "secret," in the dead of night. But in a watershed decision, Toronto's street art was legitimized in 2011, and the StreetARToronto program was born. The artists generally get permission from property owners in order to paint. The work is for the most part respected and there is very little tagging, but most of

the murals have a limited shelf life and get painted over with new work in time.

Eti worked with ward councillors Adam Vaughan and Joe Cressy, the community, Shamez Amlani of the Queen Street West Business Improvement Area, and architects Brigitte Shim and Astra Burka on long-awaited plans to improve Rush Lane with better paving, lighting, and means of garbage collection. A first step was naming lanes across the city for ease of access and emergency services. Changes were also made to provide opportunities for small businesses and new development on adjoining sites to open onto the lane. Even in its current rough state, there are frequent music performances, street-fests, and video and photo shoots. At any time of day, any day of the week, there is a steady stream of visitors, student groups, and locals checking out the art.

Toronto's laneways represent a tremendous untapped resource. There are over 250 of them, totalling almost three hundred kilometres in length, mostly in the older parts of the city. Originally designed before the car to serve as an important secondary infrastructure for carriage houses and outbuildings, service deliveries, and garbage collection, they are now being called upon to play vital new roles as the city gets denser and the population grows. The Laneway Project is actively working with various groups around the city to revitalize and adaptively reuse lanes as needed public spaces, as another way for pedestrians and cyclists to get around, and as play spaces for families with young children. As-of-right laneway housing has also been approved by the city and is starting to appear in many locations.

GETTING THERE

Located mid-block, 1.25 kilometres west of Spadina Avenue, south of and parallel to Queen Street, off of Stanley Terrace, adjacent to Trinity Bellwoods Park, with one interruption around the Loblaws store at Portland Street.

Queen streetcar, Spadina LRT, Bathurst streetcar.

Bike lanes on Richmond and Adelaide Streets nearby, local neighbourhood streets.

GRANGE PARK

A cultural
gathering point

Street, is one of our frequent destinations. A place that serves many diverse cultures, it sits on the edge of Chinatown, and is the backdrop for the Art Gallery of Ontario, OCAD University, and the University Settlement.

What is now a park started off life as the landscaped approach to The Grange, a grand manor house built by the Boulton family in 1817. It is the twelfth-oldest surviving building in Toronto and the oldest remaining brick house. In 1910 Harriet Boulton donated her estate, which included The Grange and the surrounding property, to the Art Museum of Toronto (later the Art Gallery of Ontario). In 1911 the art museum reached an agreement with the City of Toronto to make the grounds south of The Grange a public park.

At one point, Eti lived across Beverley Street from the park, where she did tai chi. Starting in 2008, Ken worked with the AGO and the local community on a skillful redesign of the park by the landscape firm PFS Studio to respond to its increased use and popularity. It has become a great year-round people place for all ages and a vital centre for the neighbourhood. It has an adventure playground and a generous dog park, but the central feature is its inviting circular common, which plays host to a great overlay of community life. Its edges provide a sweeping historical panorama of old and new structures, from the historic Grange House to the AGO to OCAD University, with the colourful stilts that support its addition, designed by architect Will Alsop. We love to sit on a linear bench facing southwest in the afternoon sun to enjoy the energy of the park and the people doing all manner of things.

Frank Gehry, the architect of the latest version of the gallery, who lived around the corner as a child, added the brilliant blue wall facing the park. We have few such examples of bold colour in our city's architecture. Another feature of the park is the powerful sculpture *Large Two Forms* by Henry Moore. For years, this was awkwardly crammed onto a street corner on the north side of the art gallery. Now it has room to breathe and be seen in the beautifully redesigned Grange Park. It is irresistible to the passersby of all ages who get up close and personal. The patina on the bronze is evidence of the many hands that have touched it.

GETTING THERE

📍 Between Beverley Street and McCaul Street, south of the Art Gallery of Ontario.

🚇 The St. Patrick subway station on subway Line 1; the Dundas, Queen, and Spadina streetcars.

🚲🚶 From all the surrounding streets, close to Chinatown centred on Spadina Avenue, and just north of Queen Street West.

KENSINGTON MARKET

An eclectic microcosm
of Toronto

KENSINGTON MARKET HAS LONG been a landing place in our evolving immigrant society, one of our first discoveries as newcomers. The land was purchased by George Taylor Denison in 1815. By the 1880s, small houses were constructed for working-class immigrant labourers from the British Isles. They were followed by waves of immigrants from elsewhere, including Jews from Eastern Europe. During the Depression, they opened stores at the front of their houses and the area became known as the "Jewish Market." By the 1930s, over sixty thousand Jews lived in and around Kensington, worshipping in over thirty synagogues. The Kiever still functions on the corner of Bellevue Square Park.

From the outset, the market featured foods and other items difficult to find elsewhere in the city. Eti has been doing her weekly shopping for decades in Carlos' House of Spices and Global Cheese. Tom of Tom's Place is a friend. Eti's daughter Mika is the proprietor of the Good Egg, a cookbook store on Augusta.

During the '50s, new waves of immigrants came from such places as the Azores, the Caribbean, and East Asia. The Vietnam War brought American draft dodgers like Ken, and during the '80s and '90s groups from Central and South America, Africa, Iran, Vietnam, and other trouble spots arrived.

Kensington has become a gathering place for artists, writers, and musicians and always has an exciting, interesting vibe. There is an annual Kensington Market Winter Solstice Festival, with groups like the Samba Squad and our friend Richard Underhill playing a post-sunset concert in nearby Alexandra Park, and Molly Johnson's intimate Kensington Market Jazz Festival. Kensington exists as a kind of "free zone," where fixed rules don't entirely apply. The area boasts laneway houses, created before the name was coined, from the 1890s, and outdoor displays of goods, illegal in other places in the city, have long been common. Pedestrians walk freely between slow-moving cars; on special Sundays cars are banned.

The market is constantly reinventing itself. Recently, there have been efforts to gentrify the neighbourhood but there is considerable pushback against this change. Eti worked with then city councillor Adam Vaughan on measures to protect Kensington's uniqueness and keep Kensington *Kensington*, and the new generation continues to be vigilant.

GETTING THERE

It fits in a tight "square" in the heart of the city, between College Street, Spadina Avenue, Dundas Street, and Bathurst Street. Most shops are located on Augusta Avenue, Baldwin Street, and Kensington Avenue.

Spadina LRT; College, Dundas, and Bathurst streetcars.

From local streets.

FRONT YARD STORIES

The element of surprise on Toronto's residential streets

ON OUR WALKS IN TORONTO'S OLDER neighbourhoods, we are constantly impressed by how people express their individuality in their small front gardens and on the porches of their homes. The houses themselves, built in different periods and coming in many sizes, shapes, and styles, are already diverse. The different flowers, herbs, and vegetables growing in the yards and other, more personal touches that further adorn these homes enliven the streets and add colour and richness for passersby to enjoy. Together, they convey a sense of neighbourliness. They say something about the spirit of Toronto and add a special "seasoning" by making the ordinary extraordinary. There is a DNA in the older neighbourhoods of our city, a spirit of live and let live, room for idiosyncrasy and fantasy, and a respect for and enjoyment of each other's differences. It is very unlike the enforced homogeneity of many new developments and the blandness of some newer house designs, which have eliminated porches or stoops, the special, sociable space between the private domestic world and the public sidewalk, leaving no room for any visible trace of the occupants. These front gardens say something about who we are, the choices we make, and how we present ourselves to the city and to each other.

A few very special examples: Out on our bikes, we suddenly came upon a remarkable fibreglass elephant at 77 Yarmouth Road. This friendly life-sized sculpture, which

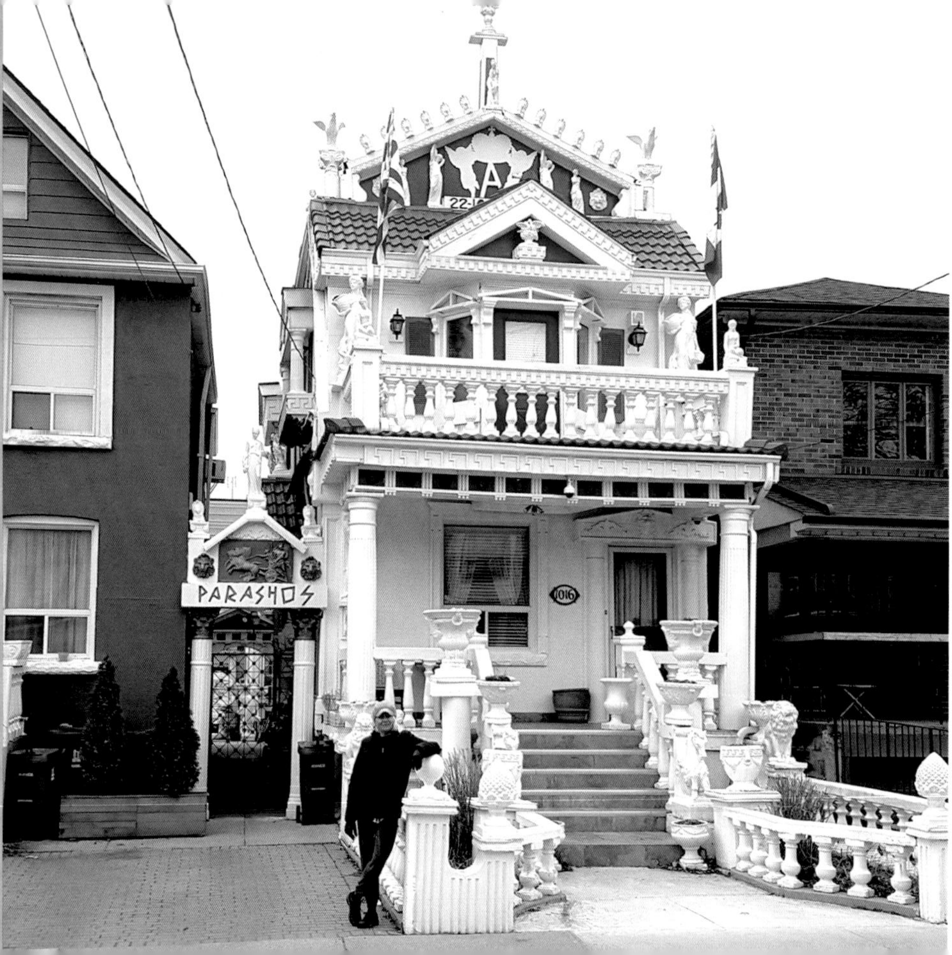
PARASHOS
1016

stands almost three metres high, was created in 1999 by Matt Donovan as part of a student thesis project at OCAD (Ontario College of Art and Design) University and given as a gift to the owner of this home. It makes the street a special place in the Christie Pits neighbourhood.

Another example, the House of Parashos at 1016 Shaw Street, is named for the man who built it over thirty years ago. Torontonians from all over the world have found unique ways to represent where they came from. This incredible house, embellished with sculptures, ornaments, and symbols honouring Greek traditions, is a standout among its neighbours.

And there is the delightful collection of treasures at 473 Clinton Street, where Albino Carreira has made the creation of an extraordinary sculpture garden his life's work ever since a jobsite accident disabled him twenty-eight years ago. Filled with intricately arranged pieces of ceramics, toys, and household objects, many donated by neighbours, it tells many stories and has become a much-loved landmark in Seaton Village.

And these are only a few of the many to discover.

GETTING THERE

Simply be on the lookout as you wander through Toronto's neighbourhoods. Some addresses are noted above but these idiosyncratic grace notes and surprises are to be found in many locations.

THE BELTLINE

An abondoned rail line becomes a revealing trail circling the city

THE BELTLINE IS A GREAT TORONTO example of "rails to trails" transformation. Today, its nine-kilometre cycling and walking trail follows the trace of an 1892 rail line that linked new suburban neighbourhoods, then north of city limits. It is one of our favourites in fall, spring, and summer.

The trail has three sections: the York Beltline Trail west of Allen Road; the Kay Gardner Beltline Park from Allen Road to Mount Pleasant Road; and the Ravine Beltline Trail, which runs south of Mount Pleasant Cemetery descending into the Don Valley at the Evergreen Brick Works. It passes through the Rosedale, Moore Park, Forest Hill, Chaplin Estates, and Fairbank neighbourhoods. Unfortunately, parts of the original rail right-of-way west of Allen Road were sold off, and to complete the original loop, it is now necessary to use city streets to make it over to the Humber Valley and down to the waterfront.

Never profitable, the passenger train service lasted for only two years. Parts of the rail line then sat unused. Over the years, a number of interested parties put forward competing plans for the use of the land. This competition resulted in one of the first public battles over the creation of biking trails in the city. Many adjacent homeowners wished to buy the land to extend their backyards, but in 1972, the land was purchased by the city as part of a land swap with Canadian National Railway.

One of the supporters of turning the railbed into a bike path was David Crombie, who was elected as mayor of Toronto soon after. Ken's Urban Design Group had a hand in making the trail a reality. The rail bridge over Yonge Street had deteriorated and was refurbished in 1993, and by 2000 the part of the trail from Allen Road to Mount Pleasant Road was designated the Kay Gardner Beltline Park after a local councillor who was a big supporter.

The mid-portion of the Beltline Trail is a magnificent tree-lined passage cutting through the heart of the city; the tree canopies touch, forming a continuous green ceiling. Gravel crunches underfoot as one walks the trail, but it is otherwise quiet, away from all traffic. There is a unique feeling of being enveloped in nature inside the city with glimpses into adjoining backyards for walkers and cyclists.

GETTING THERE

From the Don Valley at the Brick Works to Dufferin Street north of Eglinton Avenue.

Can be accessed from the Davisville subway station on subway Line 1, and bus lines including Eglinton, Dufferin, Bathurst, and Chaplin Crescent.

From the Don Valley Trail at the Evergreen Brick Works, the David Balfour Park Trail, and numerous cycle lanes on city streets crossing the Beltline.

WEST DON LANDS

A new neighbourhood
comes to life

ONE OF THE HARDEST CHALLENGES in city building is to create a new neighbourhood from scratch that has the richness and variety of ones that have grown up slowly piece by piece. While still a work in progress, the West Don Lands, also known as the Canary District — its name is taken from the historic Canary restaurant, a well-known local truck stop that operated there when it was an industrial area — is an example of how this can be done. Each time we visit, we see more signs of this neighbourhood coming to life.

The West Don Lands is filling a void and tying together historic Corktown (named for the Irish immigrant workers who lived there) to the north, and the Distillery and the St. Lawrence neighbourhoods to the west. One of the things that gives this neighbourhood real character is its history. We recently got very involved in a major community and professional effort to save the historic Dominion Foundry buildings from being demolished.

The West Don Lands neighbourhood could only be developed by solving a flooding problem first. The solution involved the creation of a park. It sits on an engineered landform that protects the downtown from flooding. It is a great example of "landscape urbanism," where landscape architecture is used to solve an engineering problem — in this case, the need to protect a large, formerly flood-prone area of downtown. Designed with Ken's input by landscape architect Michael Van Valkenburgh,

Corktown Common, with its playground, splash pads, picnic areas, and working wetlands, is extremely well used.

At its highest point, there is a stunning park pavilion designed by architect Maryann Thompson and there are great views back to the city and to the river valley. All the vegetation in the park are native species. There is a trail opening in the flood wall we often use to connect to the Don Valley Trail and the waterfront. Front Street, the spine of the neighbourhood, has an extra-wide stretch of sidewalk that is starting to attract new businesses and restaurants. The area also has a campus of George Brown College and a well-equipped YMCA.

Front Street has a number of eye-catching public artworks. One of these, the

Water Guardians, is a sculpture by Jennifer Marman and Daniel Borins. Three towering figures standing on a rubberized soft surface with waves suggesting a riverbed are illuminated at night forming a gateway. Kids love to play there; the city itself becomes a playground.

GETTING THERE

📍 Located at the east end of Front Street on the edge of the Don Valley.

🚊 504 King streetcar to the Distillery.

🚲🚶 Local streets and the Don Valley bike trail.

PORT LANDS BRIDGES

Portals to Toronto's
new frontier on the
waterfront

BRIDGES CAN BE MUCH MORE THAN just functional. They say a great deal about us. That is why we have so often been drawn to them on our walks and rides. They provide unique experiences for pedestrians and cyclists when they traverse rivers, creeks, and valleys, forming special places and unique vantage points to take in the larger scene and connect with nature and the flow of city life.

Four new bridges will soon connect downtown Toronto to Toronto's revitalized waterfront. These bridges will link to the new Villiers Island formed by extending the relocated Don River through the Port Lands. This is all part of a massive revitalization project, the largest of its kind in North America, being undertaken by Waterfront Toronto, a federal-provincial-city agency. It is overseeing the 1.25-billion-dollar project to floodproof Toronto's waterfront and transform an industrial wasteland into a vibrant, green downtown neighbourhood.

The neighbourhood, where thousands will soon live and work, will overlook a kilometre-long meandering river valley park where people can touch the water, launch small boats, and have access to multiple pedestrian and cycling paths. In 2007, Waterfront Toronto held an international design competition that looked at different configurations for the mouth of the Don as it enters Toronto Harbour. Ken collaborated with Michael Van Valkenburgh Associates on the winning competition entry, which set this whole effort in motion, and later with the winners of another international design competition for the bridges with Entuitive and Grimshaw Architects. Though each bridge is different, with its own distinguishing colour, they form an aesthetically unified family providing the Port Lands neighbourhood with light rail, vehicular, cycle, and pedestrian connections.

These colourful and inviting bridges were intentionally made wider for pedestrians and cyclists and provide ideal "people places" to pause and look out over the Don River and observe its seasonal changes, rising and falling, as it meanders through the broad band of surrounding parkland where it enters Toronto Harbour.

Integrated night lighting will illuminate the ribs and slender shell-like forms of the bridges. They will become a visual symbol of Toronto's evolution. We have really enjoyed seeing these beautiful bridges float into view on barges and fit into place.

GETTING THERE

📍 Located surrounding the new Villiers Island at the new Cherry Street crossings of the Keating Channel, the Don River mouth, and at Lake Shore Boulevard.

🚇 A work in progress, eventually via the Waterfront LRT extension; for now the 172 Queens Quay bus.

🚲🚶 On the Martin Goodman Trail to Cherry Beach.

THE DON VALLEY

Reclaiming a
river valley

THE DON RIVER VALLEY, THE CITY'S deepest and widest ravine, feels removed from the city and tells a compelling story of "lost and found." It cuts a wide swath through Toronto from the Oak Ridges Moraine in the north to Lake Ontario.

Humans first arrived in the valley approximately 12,500 years ago, most likely as nomadic hunters. The river's Indigenous name is Wonscotonach, an Anishnaabemowin phrase meaning "the river coming from the burnt grounds," which might refer to an earlier forest fire to the north. Lieutenant Governor Simcoe called it Don River because the wide valley reminded him of the River Don in Yorkshire.

The European settlers immediately began to exploit the river's power, setting up mills and factories. Polluted effluent from the growing city quickly began to turn the Don and its marshy mouth into a polluted hazard. The railway followed and then in the mid-twentieth century the Don Valley Parkway was brutally shoehorned into the valley to serve growing commuter traffic. By the 1960s the Don River Valley was a neglected mess. In 1969, there was even a much celebrated "Funeral for the Don" to highlight its sorry state. A citizen advisory body, the Task Force to Bring Back the Don formed with a mandate and vision to make the Don "clean, green, and accessible."

When we are there, we sense the "healing of nature" that is underway, the cleanup of the river itself, and the new planting on its banks and slopes. Wildlife is returning.

When Ken worked for the city, he introduced a trail from the waterfront up to Pottery Road, filling in a missing piece in a network of well-used trails that link the waterfront to Edwards Gardens and Taylor Creek and beyond. With Evergreen Brick Works, the city has now also launched ambitious plans for a Don River Valley park (named Wonscotonach Parklands) that will stretch for seven kilometres through the valley. A great feature is the beautiful Prince Edward Viaduct, built in 1918 but designed to accommodate the subway that would not be built until some forty-five years later. The parklands have also become a place for public art. One installation we enjoy near the base of the Prince Edward Viaduct is *Monsters for Beauty, Permanence and Individuality*. Artist Duane Linklater, an Omaskêko Cree from Moose Cree First Nation, created concrete castings from fourteen distinctive gargoyles that used to adorn Toronto's buildings and placed them on the trail south of the Evergreen Brick Works for us to discover.

GETTING THERE

The Don Valley and its tributaries slice through the heart of Toronto from the Oak Ridges Moraine to Lake Ontario.

By subway, Line 2 to Broadview station; by streetcar, the 504 King car to Broadview station.

From the Don Valley Trail from the waterfront; trails from Riverdale Farm, Rosedale Ravine, the east end of Wellesley Street, and Pottery Road.

TRINITY BELLWOODS PARK

A neighbourhood park with the ghost of a creek

TRINITY BELLWOODS PARK HAS A BIT of everything: a community recreation centre; popular outdoor tennis courts; an outdoor skating rink; a volleyball court; field space for soccer, football, and rugby; and three softball fields. Trails weave through the park every which way for pedestrians and cyclists. With all of these, it's little wonder that Trinity Bellwoods is constantly animated, active, and lively, enjoyed by people of all ages. It is a favourite hangout for groups of young people, who pick their spots among the trees, and it served as a vital outdoor living room during the time of the Covid lockdown.

The park has an irregular shape and topography, a result of the fact that most of it lies in the trace of the original Garrison Creek Ravine. In the 1950s, Garrison Creek, which emptied into Lake Ontario beside Fort York, was entirely buried in a storm sewer. The ravine was backfilled at the north end, an action that raised the surface of the park to almost the height of Dundas Street. But even if the creek is no longer visible, its presence remains. The steep drop from this upper level to the lower part forms a "bowl" that has become a popular toboggan run in winter and the city's largest designated "off-leash" dog park.

It was once the site of Trinity College (from which the park takes part of its name), which opened in 1852. The college was eventually moved to the University of Toronto campus. The original buildings were sold to the City of Toronto and mostly demolished in the early 1950s, but the grand stone and iron gates remain as an entrance to the park on Queen Street, facing Strachan Avenue. There is a seniors' residence, John Gibson House, which occupies the former St. Hilda's College building (a women's residence of Trinity College). The building, which dates back to 1899, still overlooks the northern half of the park.

This beloved and well-used park, which we often use as a shortcut between Queen and Dundas Streets, provides a year-round space for a welcome break in the fabric of the city. In 2001, the Friends of Trinity Bellwoods Park was formed to coordinate volunteer activities and provide input to the city on maintaining the park for its intensive use and plans for what will come next.

GETTING THERE

📍 (790 Queen Street West) Bordered by Queen Street West to the south and Dundas Street West to the north, Crawford Street to the west, and Gore Vale Avenue to the east.

🚃 Accessible via the Queen Street (Strachan Avenue stop) and Dundas Street (Shaw Street stop) streetcars.

🚲🚶 Local streets.

RONCESVALLES (A.K.A. "RONCY")

A one-sided main street, the exception that proves the rule

RONCESVALLES AVENUE GIVES ITS name to a neighbourhood, its nickname being "Roncy." Roncesvalles ("valley of thorns" in Spanish) runs from the intersection of King and Queen Streets in the south to Dundas Street in the north and connects the popular Junction neighbourhood to Lake Ontario.

What makes this neighbourhood special is the commercial strip that runs the full length, composed of a variety of small, independently owned businesses in low-rise structures built in the first half of the twentieth century. These include gift shops, pharmacies, health food stores, fresh produce shops, clothing and shoe stores, cafés and restaurants, book and music stores, video stores, art shops, hardware stores, and law offices. Another neighbourhood feature is the popular repertory Revue Cinema, which closed temporarily but reopened as a community not-for-profit operation of the Revue Film Society.

Conventional wisdom has it that one-sided main streets can't work, but Roncesvalles, with shops on only its east side, is an exception.

Roncesvalles is an area with a rich Indigenous history. A trail (now Indian Road) was an ancient path for the Mississaugas of the Credit First Nation, leading north from Lake Ontario. Following European colonization, farm lots were given to prominent Toronto families. The railways came in the mid-nineteenth century, and the foot of

Roncesvalles became a commercial and transportation hub, with a train station, a bus depot, and a streetcar loop. It was well connected to Sunnyside Amusement Park on Lake Ontario, but after the park was demolished for the Gardiner Expressway in 1955 and the Sunnyside intersection bypassed, there was a decline in commerce.

The wealthy moved away, but the area still remained largely middle class, attracting an influx of immigrants, especially from Poland. In fact, it became the centre of the Polish community in Toronto, with restaurants, delicatessens, and shops specializing in Polish goods. Today, people from all over the globe have gravitated to the neighbourhood, demonstrating the city's remarkable capacity to absorb mix and diversity. Sidewalk life on Roncy is vibrant.

In 2012, Roncesvalles was named one of eight finalists in the Canadian Institute of Planners' (CIP) Great Places in Canada contest — the only Toronto neighbourhood to make the list.

GETTING THERE

📍 The street runs for approximately 1.6 kilometres between the Junction to the north and Lake Ontario to the south.

🚋 South on the 504 Dundas streetcar from Dundas West subway station on subway Line 2.

🚲🚶 Martin Goodman Trail to the south with a bridge over the Gardiner Expressway, Bloor Street bike lane to the north, and local streets.

HIGH
PARK

Our big incity park
from Bloor Street
to the lake

HIGH PARK IS THE CLOSEST THING Toronto has to a generous "central park." At 160 hectares, it is the second largest municipal park in Toronto, after the Toronto Islands. It carves out a large green space and demonstrates the special value of such a large park inside the city, free and open to all. We and many Torontonians keep gravitating to it. It offers a real experience of wild nature in the city for many who cannot easily travel long distances.

The park mirrors in microcosm the topography of Toronto with two deep ravines extending the full north–south length of the park. Creeks feed Grenadier Pond, a large body of water located in the southwestern corner. The park is still big enough to get "lost" in, out of sight of the buildings that surround it. It reflects the changing seasons and truly provides something for everyone, including relatively undisturbed nature with abundant flora and fauna.

High Park was opened to the public in 1876 through an act of philanthropy based on a bequest from John George Howard after his successful career as an architect, engineer, and land surveyor for the City of Toronto. The park is part of the traditional territories of the Wendat, Haudenosaunee, Anishinaabe, and the Mississaugas of the Credit. According to the Taiaiako'n Historical Preservation Society, there are fifty-seven ancient Indigenous Peoples' burial mounds in the park.

While the park is penetrated by roads, these are increasingly reserved for pedestrians and cyclists at busy times. This beautiful mixed recreational and natural city park contains sporting, cultural, and educational facilities; gardens; playgrounds; and a zoo. One-third of it remains in a natural state. Amongst the many native species that can be found in this untouched area is a rare oak savannah.

In spring, the blossoms on the cherry trees found on the hillside overlooking Grenadier Pond are a great attraction. During the summer months, a natural amphitheatre on a hillside directly to the east of the Grenadier Cafe hosts selected plays performed by the Canadian Stage company, including the annual Shakespeare in High Park, as well as concerts. And there are always small surprises, like *Spirit in a Tree*. Walking one of the paths, we discovered a striking face carved into a tree trunk (see page 92). This work by artist Colin Partridge was created in 2006 when he was commissioned by the City of Toronto.

GETTING THERE

📍 Located west of downtown and north of Humber Bay, it stretches south from Bloor Street West to the Queensway between Parkside Drive and Ellis Park Road.

🚇 One block south of High Park station on subway Line 2.

🚲🚶 North: Bloor–Danforth bike lane; south: one block north of Martin Goodman Trail on the waterfront.

HUMBER BAY SHORES PARK

Celebrating the mouth
of the Humber River

ONE OF OUR FAVOURITE SPOTS BY bike or walking, winter or summer, is Humber Bay Shores Park, located just west across the Humber Bay Arch Bridge. This nineteen-hectare park was developed by the Toronto and Region Conservation Authority as part of a string of new parks along the Etobicoke shoreline connected by the Martin Goodman Trail. The park extends out into Lake Ontario. It is protected from wind and wave action by armoured points shaping its graceful curvilinear forms. It provides great 360-degree views of water and land and a place to get away from the crowds.

The park adds width to what was a narrow band of land and today provides a welcoming "front" for an emerging high-rise neighbourhood. The initially isolated cluster of high-rise towers located at the mouth of the Humber is becoming more a part of the city and a genuine neighbourhood, with more and more new restaurants and outdoor cafés, where we often stop. It is a popular destination for both locals and visitors.

Entering the Humber Bay Shores Park is like passing through a gateway to another world, a unique city park literally in the lake, surrounded by water on all sides. It is easy to get lost in nature within the web of trails, some very narrow and surrounded by vegetation. Suddenly, you come upon openings with great views out to the water and the downtown core to the east. It is almost possible in this newly created patch of land to imagine what the Lake Ontario shoreline might have been before the city developed.

It is remarkable how nature has taken over what was essentially artificial land created through landfill. Several habitat restoration projects have been introduced, including the planting of Carolinian trees and shrubs, the establishment of wild-flower meadows, and a warm-water fish habitat and wetland. The park is also a popular destination to view migrating birds and is listed as one of the top spots for birdwatching in Toronto. You can see a wide variety of overwintering ducks. There is also the Humber Bay Butterfly Habitat, which provides habitat for native butter-flies. As well, there is a wonderful length of beach with natural art in the form of sculptural driftwood.

The pebble beach on the south shore is a hidden treasure, a great place for picnick-ing, swimming, and wading, including for families with kids.

GETTING THERE

📍 Located along the Martin Goodman Trail west of the Humber River.

🚋 The 501, 510, and 511 streetcars to Lake Shore Boulevard.

🚲🚶 On the Martin Goodman Trail, and from Park Lawn Road.

HUMBER BAY ARCH BRIDGE

A welcoming window
to Lake Ontario on the
Waterfront Trail

WE ARE IRRESISTIBLY DRAWN TO THE water, the city's place of origin on Lake Ontario. We like to move along the water's edge, experiencing the open horizon in all seasons. On a clear day, it's sometimes possible to see the shorelines of Niagara-on-the-Lake and New York state. From the Humber Bay Arch Bridge, the panorama is spectacular. Looking east to downtown, we can pick out the CN Tower and SkyDome (a.k.a. the Rogers Centre); the constantly changing skyline of the city, with its many towering condos and office buildings; and even specific neighbourhoods. The bridge is also a fantastic place for people-watching, as many others stop there, too, to take in the view.

This iconic, graceful, arched, cable-stayed bridge over the mouth of the Humber River is one of the truly special landing places on the waterfront. Standing under the arches of the bridge, you almost feel like you are in a cathedral, and the sensation of the flow of the river is fantastic. Looking down from the bridge — upriver or south to the lake — we enjoy watching the traffic of canoes, kayaks, paddleboards, and occasional motorboats, and the swooping movement of waterfowl of all kinds. The colourful chairs and grassy hillside found on Sheldon Lookout, an outcropping into the lake on the west bank of the river mouth, provide a great place to view the bridge.

The bridge forms a critical link on the Martin Goodman Trail, which is part of the Waterfront Trail, the multi-use pathway that will eventually parallel the entire north shore of Lake Ontario. It is one of our favourite destinations for a bike ride, the perfect stopping point if you're taking a trip across the western beaches and eventually out to New Toronto, Long Branch, and Port Credit. The Humber Bay Arch Bridge sits at the start of the Toronto Carrying Place trail, an ancient Indigenous trading route leading north up the Humber River. The bridge, designed in 1994 by Montgomery Sisam Architects of Toronto and Delcan bridge engineers, features design elements such as carved turtles and canoes in the abutments that evoke this Indigenous heritage.

We are almost never alone on the bridge as it is such a tempting place to pause and appreciate the scene. From below, at river level on the trail, it is fun to watch the endless flow of pedestrians and cyclists in profile, forming a kinetic sculpture that is always in movement.

GETTING THERE

 Located at the mouth of the Humber River on the Martin Goodman Trail.

 Accessible via the King or Queen streetcars to Ellis Avenue on the Queensway and then a short walk south.

 Just follow the Martin Goodman Trail on the western beaches.

OLD MILL BRIDGE

A perch on the
Humber River valley

AT THE WESTERN END OF BLOOR West Village, one of our favourite city walks, Bloor Street curves and dips down into the Humber River valley. Travelling by car, you are hardly aware you are crossing the river on a bridge, but walking a few blocks north there is another very special river crossing with a storied history.

The Old Mill Bridge connecting Old Mill Road to Catherine Street was designed by engineer Frank Barber in 1916 after numerous other bridges were swept away by flooding and ice floes. This elegant concrete and stone bridge seems small and delicate by today's standards, but it was solidly built to withstand the power of the river. Narrow and short with a gentle camber or rise, it is an ideal place to look over the river valley. The narrow width makes traffic slow down for pedestrians and cyclists. From here, you can see the valley's changes in all seasons, from salmon jumping the weirs to make their way to spawning grounds in the fall to the ice breakup in the spring.

The Humber River valley trails, lined with parks, meander up- and downriver and are accessible from this point. These generous parks exist because in 1954 Hurricane Hazel caused massive destruction in the Humber River valley. The river rose with incredible force into surrounding communities. Houses were swept away, and many lives were lost. This led to the creation of the Toronto and Region Conservation Authority and the protection of the river and creek valleys that have given us a magnificent ravine park system occupying 17 percent of Toronto's land area.

Before the arrival of British settlers in the late eighteenth century, this section of the Humber River was used by numerous First Nations to travel from Lake Ontario to the north. The settlers established the King's Mill (now the site of the Old Mill Toronto, a popular hotel, spa, and restaurant). Over time, a total of 164 mills were set up to take advantage of the water's power. The problem was that the demand for wood led to deforestation along the river and the removal of trees and undergrowth reduced the land's ability to absorb water, resulting in increasingly severe floods. Standing on the bridge looking up- and downriver we are reminded that we live in nature and have to recognize and work with its power.

GETTING THERE

📍 Located a few blocks north of Bloor Street, this is the Humber River crossing on Old Mill Road in the Kingsway neighbourhood.

🚇 Not far from Old Mill subway station on subway Line 2.

🚲🚶 Local neighbourhood streets.

LESLIE STREET SPIT

Nature takes over
a barren landfill

FIVE KILOMETRES EAST FROM DOWNtown Toronto, a walk or bike ride away, we come upon wild nature on the Leslie Street Spit. This long, slender finger of land stretches five kilometres into Lake Ontario, with "lobes" enclosing small bays and wetlands. We are drawn to the stark contrast of "city in nature" and "nature in the city."

This "spit" is a product of a failed plan to create an outer harbour. Landfilling for a breakwater by the Toronto Harbour Commission began in the 1950s to expand shipping on the Great Lakes through the St. Lawrence Seaway, but a new generation of container ships were too big to navigate the locks, and cargo traffic shifted to east coast ports.

Although conceived as an extension of the harbour, the spit has evolved into a nature preserve and passive recreation area colonized by a wide variety of flora and fauna — an urban wilderness never in the city's plans. The spit's new status was secured by a citizens' group, known as Friends of the Spit, that advocated to naturalize the site. The northern half has been designated as Tommy Thompson Park, named after a former Toronto parks commissioner.

Nature has taken over, and when we go there, we enter another world. We leave traffic behind — the Leslie Street Spit is a car-free area when the park is open. The views back to the city are amazing, especially from the lighthouse at the tip where

LESLIE STREET SPIT   111

the power of wind and waves is impressive. Visitors have created a constantly changing "sculpture garden" made from discarded construction materials, concrete blocks, bricks, tiles, slabs, and reinforcing rods — all part of the landfill.

There is a touch of mystery in this emerging landscape where nature is taking over on new ground formed from the detritus of the city. Parts of the spit have been taken over by seagulls and cormorants, both establishing colonies and nesting grounds. More than three hundred species of birds have been identified, forty-five of which breed there. As a result, it has been designated as an Important Bird Area by Nature Canada. The spit teems with new life in spring. Just off the trail, we discovered a

hidden cove ringed by tall reeds with a beaver lodge. As we were standing there admiring the view, we saw the beaver swimming toward the lodge.

GETTING THERE

📍 Located at the foot of Leslie Street at the intersection with Unwin Avenue.

🚌 Number 83 Bus on Leslie Street to Commissioners Street and then a seven-minute walk.

🚲🚶 On the Martin Goodman Trail.

THE BEACH

A historic neighbourhood
where the city embraces
the lake

FOR THE MOST PART, TORONTO HAS not allowed easy public access to Lake Ontario. The Beach is a rare exception. Also known as "the Beaches," it is a waterfront community stretching from Victoria Park Avenue to Coxwell Avenue with a continuous sandy beachfront bounded by the iconic R.C. Harris Water Treatment Plant (celebrated in Michael Ondaatje's *In the Skin of a Lion*) and Woodbine Beach. A three-kilometre boardwalk, paralleled by the Martin Goodman Trail, runs along its length.

The neighbourhood was originally a heavily wooded area dotted with summer cottages, eventually winterized to become year-round residences. The Beach became a streetcar suburb. In the early 1900s, to protect the shoreline from erosion, wooden groynes were constructed, which is why the beach is public space today. The boardwalk was opened to the public in 1932.

The boardwalk forms a walking "loop" with Queen Street, lined with independent specialty stores, cafés, and restaurants, just a few hundred metres away to the north. The side streets have a great mix of housing, often now referred to as the "missing middle" — fourplexes, semi-detached homes, row houses, and low-rise apartment buildings. Together, these serve a variety of households and lifestyles.

Kew Gardens, running from the beach up to Queen Street, is the neighbourhood's central community park. It features a library, baseball diamond, hockey rink, and lawn bowling. The parks and beach have long been a favourite picnic area for large multi-generational newcomer families and locals. Special things happen on the beach in addition to swimming, boating, windsurfing, kite flying, and beach volleyball. In the winter, the Winter Stations art installations take over the lifeguard stations. There is also a hugely popular summer Beaches International Jazz Festival on Queen Street, drawing thousands.

The boardwalk expands out into wider green spaces, the graceful sloping lawns of the R.C. Harris Water Treatment Plant in the east and Woodbine Beach and Ashbridges Bay extending a generous parkland peninsula out into the lake in the west.

The Beach is an active, liveable community — walkable, pedestrian and cycle friendly, well-loved by locals and visitors.

GETTING THERE

The eastern end of the old City of Toronto on the Lake Ontario shoreline.

The 501 Queen streetcar takes you right there with a number of stops from Woodbine Avenue to Neville Park; the 64 bus also takes you from the Main Street subway station on subway Line 2 right to Queen Street; the 92 south bus from Woodbine station on Line 2 provides another way to reach The Beach.

The Beach is right on the eastern end of the Martin Goodman Trail that traverses the Toronto waterfront and is an easy walk down any of the neighbourhood streets from Queen Street.

THE GUILD OF ALL ARTS (CLARK CENTRE FOR THE ARTS)

Rescued architectural fragments form a unique sculpture garden

ROUGHLY SEVENTEEN KILOMETRES east of downtown, high up on the Scarborough Bluffs overlooking Lake Ontario, there is a remarkable thirty-six-hectare park containing the Guild of All Arts (now the Clark Centre for the Arts). The bluffs stretch for about fifteen kilometres from Toronto's Eastern Beaches to East Point Park. This dramatic feature was produced by the accumulation of sediment over twelve thousand years ago and has since been shaped by wind and water erosion from Lake Ontario.

In 1932, visionary philanthropists Spencer and Rosa Clark established an artist collective on the property, which focused on their interests in arts and crafts, health and nutrition, alternative education, and co-operative movements. By the time of the Second World War, it had become the Guild of All Arts. The Clarks built homes and workshops for artists, such as The Studio. The Clarks also began collecting architectural remnants, stone carvings, and statuary from the Victorian, beaux arts, and Gothic revival buildings at King and Bay, the heart of the Financial District, which were being demolished to make way for the new buildings constructed in Toronto's explosive postwar growth. These rescued treasures were reassembled in the gardens.

Ken met and assisted Spencer and Rosa when he was director of the Architecture and Urban Design department at the City of Toronto. There was a lack of formal heritage protection at the time, and the modern movement that dominated architectural taste at the time had little sympathy for these structures, which were replaced by gleaming new bank towers. Without the Clarks' intervention, these irreplaceable artefacts would no doubt have ended up in landfills. Here they are in a natural setting along with some newer works.

The park has become popular for wedding parties and for those who simply come to enjoy the day with their families. The Guild Festival Theatre performs in the famous Greek Theatre, made from salvaged marble columns from the 1912 Bank of Toronto Building. There is something very special about seeing these fragments from downtown Toronto in a park on the bluffs laid out as a garden.

In 1999, the park was designated a heritage property by the Heritage Canada Foundation, and in 2014 the City of Toronto developed a management plan to preserve this special park for public use.

GETTING THERE

📍 On the Scarborough Bluffs overlooking Lake Ontario in the Guildwood area of Scarborough.

🚆 GO Train from downtown to Eglinton Station and a ride on the 116 bus to Guildwood Parkway.

🚲🚶 Not easily accessible — a twenty-five-kilometre bike ride from downtown on Kingston Road or a circuitous route on the Martin Goodman Trail on neighbourhood streets.

ACKNOWLEDGEMENTS

WE WANT TO THANK THE GREAT TEAM AT DUNDURN, IN PARTICULAR associate publisher Kathryn Lane for her help and support in making this project a reality, and our editor, Dominic Farrell, for his close attention to our words to help us tell the stories.

During the time of Covid, we all came to see the incalculable value of public spaces, but they don't just happen by themselves — they need care and support. We want to express our gratitude to the four organizations we have been privileged to be on the boards of that play key roles in advocating for public life in our city: first and foremost, 8 80 Cities, our valued partner in producing this book; and also the Bentway, Park People, and Myseum.

We also want to thank organizations like Waterfront Toronto, the Toronto and Region Conservation Authority, and the City of Toronto itself for the great work they do in creating and maintaining many of the wonderful places we write about.

And finally, thanks go to all the unsung heroes, the civil society actors who tirelessly advocate for safer and better places for people of all ages and abilities to walk and cycle in our city.

INDEX

ABOUT THE AUTHORS

KEN AND ETI GREENBERG ARE PROUD IMMIGRANTS TO CANADA and passionate Torontonians. They have lived in downtown Toronto on Victoria Memorial Square for the past twenty-five years. Between them they have four children, three of whom live in Toronto, and seven grandchildren.

Ken was born in New York City. Trained as an architect and urban designer, he founded and led the City of Toronto's Division of Architecture and Urban Design for ten years. He has since played a pivotal role on public and private projects throughout North America and Europe. He has taught at many universities in Canada and the United States and has been involved in many grassroots and community initiatives. One of the founders of the Bentway, he is also on the board of Myseum. Through a donation with Eti, a current board member, he launched the Public Space Incubator project with Park People. A frequent writer for periodicals, he is the author of *Walking Home: The Life and Lessons of a City Builder* and *Toronto Reborn*. He is the recipient of the 2010 American Institute of Architects Thomas Jefferson Award and the 2014 Sustainable Buildings Canada Lifetime Achievement Award, and is an honorary member of the Ontario Association of Landscape Architects. In 2019, he was selected as a Member of the Order of Canada, and in 2020 was awarded a Doctor of Laws, *honoris causa*, from the University of Toronto.

Born and raised in Haifa, Israel, Eti lived in France, outside Geneva, New York City, and Jerusalem before settling in Toronto. Passionate about cities, she and Ken regularly walk and bike around Toronto, exploring the city's many remarkable places and discovering its hidden treasures. Eti has managed Toronto's Euclid Theatre, acted as an art dealer for Israeli conceptual art, and worked for two Toronto city councillors. She has practised as a shiatsu and acupuncture therapist and teaches tai chi. In the office of Councillor Adam Vaughan, she developed several special projects, including a community mapping system and a "report card" for assessing redevelopment proposals, which is now widely used. She worked on the plan for improvements to Rush Lane and sits on the boards of Park People and 8 80 Cities. In the spring of 2023, she started teaching at the Bentway. As she notes, "Through this work I have become even more involved in and enthusiastic about our remarkable city and how it is evolving. I want to share with others the experience of our walks and bike rides in the areas of the city I have come to know well."

ABOUT 8 80 CITIES

8 80 CITIES IS A NON-PROFIT ORGANIZATION based in Toronto, Canada. Their mission is to ignite action and challenge the status quo to create healthier, more equitable, and sustainable cities for all people. They are guided by the simple but powerful idea that if everything we do in our cities is great for an eight-year-old and an eighty-year-old, then it will be better for everyone. 8 80 Cities has a vision to create healthy, happy, and sustainable cities for people to grow up and grow old in, where all people have the right to safe and active mobility, welcoming and accessible public spaces, and inclusive city building processes.

Over the last seventeen years 8 80 Cities has worked in over three hundred cities around the world, sparking change and taking bold action. They believe in the transformative power of public space in advancing health and well-being, equity and justice, and climate action. Their program design seeks to centre equity-deserving communities, and their work with systemically excluded communities has underscored their emphasis on empathy, inclusion, and social solidarity. They advance their mission through grant programs, participatory research, advocacy, and the innovative 8 80 services.

For more information visit 880cities.org.